Songs of the
Sixth Dalai Lama

Songs of the
Sixth Dalai Lama

K.Dhondup

LIBRARY OF TIBETAN WORKS & ARCHIVES

ISBN: 81-85102-11-2

Published by the Library of Tibetan Works and Archives, Dharamsala, H. P. (India) and printed at Indraprastha Press (CBT), 4 Bahadurshah Zafar Marg, New Delhi 110002.

Contents

Publisher's Note

Tsangyang Gyatsho, the Sixth Dalai Lama remains a timeless enigma in the annals of the Dalai Lamas of Tibet, the highest institution of reincarnation in the whole of Central Asia.

Radiant and varied as a rainbow, Tsangyang Gyatsho was a deeply spiritual mystic of transcendental attainment in tantra in the eyes of the initiated and a perfect lover of wine and women in the eyes of the ordinary. Of his varied writings, his songs remain the most accessible and popular, and of late there has been a renewed interest in the life and times of the Sixth Dalai Lama as a figure unique in the chequered history of Tibet.

Songs of the Sixth Dalai Lama is now being translated into more foreign languages. This third edition of the English translation celebrates the enduring popularity of the Sixth Dalai Lama's songs and also commemorates the tragic and untimely demise of the talented author and translator, Mr K Dhondup, earlier this year.

Gyatsho Tshering
Director

Dec. 1995

Tsangyang Gyatso
The Rebel Dalai Lama

> White crane!
> Lend me your wings
> I will not fly far
> From Lithang, I shall return.

So wrote a desolate and lonely Tsangyang Gyatso, the Sixth Dalai Lama, to a lady-friend of his in Shol town in 1706, when he was being forcibly taken away to China by the Mongol soldiers of the Qosot Lhazang Khan—away from his people and the Potala palace. No one at that time understood the message contained in the song nor did anyone suspect that the young Dalai Lama had decided to end his earthly manifestation and yield the Tibetan spiritual and temporal realm to the care of the next Dalai Lama. But when that very year the sad and shocking news of the "disappearance" or more probably the "murder" of Tsangyang Gyatso at Gunga-Nor lake spread across the Tibetan landscape, the secret meaning of the last of his many songs dawned on the grief-stricken and bewildered Tibetan masses who dearly longed for his presence during a turbulent turn of history, and anxiously looked towards Lithang for the next reincarnation.

The short and tragic life and loves of Tsangyang Gyatso have defied definition and conjured up strange inspirations and misconceptions in the minds of millions who find delight in his songs, nostalgia in his loves and tragedy in his brief role as the Dalai Lama, the supreme spiritual and temporal institution that has led and struggled for the survival of the Tibetan nation and race ever since Gedun Drupa was recognised as the first earthly manifestation of Bodhisattva Avalokiteshvara in the 15th century till the present Tenzin Gyatso, the Fourteenth Dalai Lama, who from his exile base in Dharamsala in India is waging a relentless struggle for the ultimate independence of Tibet.

As Tsangyang Gyatso was the Sixth Dalai Lama, many find it difficult to understand his seemingly dissolute life, his many loves, his wine songs and above all, his escape from the precincts of the holy Potala to Lhasa and Shol where tavern maids and mistresses eagerly awaited his arrival and presence. So remote was Tibet and still more so the fabled city of forbidden Lhasa wih its magnificent Potala and the divine Dalai Lamas that fertile and imaginative Western minds eagerly indulged in creating fantasies about the distant Lhasa and the mystic Dalai Lamas. From among these, the rumoured lifestyles of the Sixth Dalai Lama, exported to Europe through the writings of Ippolito Desideri and other missionaries, became in the early 1830s the subject matter of a two-volume anti-religion novel entitled *Mahaguru* by the German radical-liberal writer Karl Gutzkone. Partly misinformed by *Mahaguru*, Karl Marx, in a leading article in no. 179 of the *Kolnische Zeitung*, cited the institution of the Dalai Lama as an example of totalitarian theocracy representing God on earth.

But young Tsangyang Gyatso was recognised as the Dalai Lama and brought up to suit the institution in a difficult and conflicting time under abnormal circumstances. In an attempt to partially understand his ambiguous and extraordinary history, it is necessary to evaluate the events and the diverse but dominating personalities who were crucial in their influence on the times and life of young Tsangyang Gyatso.

* * * * *

After defeating the last Tsangpa ruler Karma Tenkyong Wangpo in 1642 at Shigatse, Gushri Khan, the bearded Qosot Mongol prince and the Desi (regent) Sonam Chophel finally succeeded in unifying Tibet under the rule of Ngawang Losang

Gyatso, the Great Fifth Dalai Lama, who became the first Dalai Lama to assume full spiritual and secular control over the whole of Tibet. In 1675, at the age of 73, Gushri Khan died in Lhasa. The very next year, Desi Sonam Chophel died. Sangay Gyatso, only 27 years old in 1679, was appointed the regent following the resignation of Desi Losang Jinpa. In 1682, at 68, the Fifth Dalai Lama passed away, leaving the whole reign of temporal and spiritual administration in the hands of Desi Sangay Gyatso.

Trained in both secular and spiritual matters by his uncle Desi Trinlay Gyatso, Sangay Gyatso, popularly referred to as "Desi Goleb" (flat-headed regent) was an ambitious man of wide interests and excellent scholarship. His numerous works on history, medicine, astrology and music etc. won him scholarly recognition, and his accuracy in archery and musical talents, especially *piwang* (Tibetan lute), endeared him to his friends and the people alike. A tireless and efficient administrator, he regularly paid personal visits to the numerous courts and offices under his supervision. Conscious of the needs and aspirations of the common people, Desi Sangay often visited the drinking shops and public places in masquerades to gather public opinion on his administration. Of his numerous masquerades, there is a story that once the disguised Desi questioned a monk *Dob-dob* for the latter's opinion on the *Deba-shung* (Tibetan Government). In reply, the *Dob-dob* reportedly told the disguised Desi: "*Deba-shung* is the concern of Desi Goleb. Our concern is to drink *chang* (wine) hidden under my bed." A great lover of learning and administration, Desi Sangay was at the other extreme a lover of wine, women and music who turned unscrupulous, scheming and ruthless when the time and situation demanded.

Though the Fifth Dalai Lama passed away in 1682, this fact was concealed from the people, Mongol princes and the

Manchu emperor by Desi Sangay for about 15 years. It was announced by Desi that the Dalai Lama had retreated into meditation for an indefinite period, while within the inner circle he went to great lengths to guard the secret closely. It is also said that the Fifth Dalai Lama himself wished his demise to be kept secret as he feared that the news might hinder the construction and completion of the Potala palace then underway, and enable and encourage the Manchus to infiltrate and sow seeds of dissension among the various Mongol tribes around Kokonor who owed their total allegiance to the Dalai Lama and protected the Tibetan empire from Manchu clutches.

Whatever justifications in the reasons forwarded by Desi Sangay for concealing the demise of the Dalai Lama, the Lhasa administration was maintained admirably in the normal and usual way to impress people and visitors alike that all was well and fine. Rituals signifying the Dalai Lama's meditation were performed daily. Meals were taken into the ante-chamber as usual. The Dalai Lama's seal was used on all official transactions. On important occasions, the Dalai Lama's ceremonial gown was placed on the throne in the audience hall and all officials followed the routine as though the Dalai Lama was physically present. However, when important Mongol devotees and princes arrived from Mongolia to pay their respects to the Dalai Lama, the Desi could not refuse them audience outright. At such critical times, an elderly monk named Tasrab from *Namgyal Dratsang*, who slightly resembled the Fifth Dalai Lama in physical appearance, was made to receive the guests in the ceremonial robes, an eye-shade and a hat, most probably to conceal the fact that the monk-imposter lacked the baldness and piercing round eyes of the Fifth Dalai Lama. Placed in such extraordinary circumstances, it required the ruthless genius of one of the most intelligent Tibetans to keep such an important secret for so long. When sometimes the

monk from *Namgyal Dratsang*, bored with his forced impris-
onment and scared of his unusual role, tried to escape from the
Potala, Desi Sangay entreated, beat and most often bribed the
monk to stay to fulfil his unusual role of acting as the Fifth
Dalai Lama. In his frenzied determination to maintain the
secret, Desi Sangay is said to have murdered both the medium
of the Nechung oracle Tsewang Palbar and the latter's mother
for getting wind of the secret during Desi's frequent consultations with the oracle in the nerve-wracking suspense of running
the Tibetan administrative show without the presence of the
Dalai Lama.

It would be an unfair judgement to maintain that Desi
Sangay Gyatso was only interested in keeping the Fifth Dalai
Lama's demise a secret to prolong his personal rule. Immedi-
ately after the Fifth Dalai Lama's passing away, Desi Sangay
had started the search for the discovery of the Fifth's reincarnation and had despatched trusted officials to various parts of
the country, who pretended to be in search of reincarnations
other than that of the Dalai Lama.

In 1685, one search party reported that an extraordinary
son born supernaturally to father Rigdzin Tashi and mother
Tsewang Lhamo on 1st March 1683, in the land of *Mon*
(Tawang) seemed to be the reincarnation of the Fifth Dalai
Lama, as the child had successfully stood all the preliminary
tests performed by Chosje Zilnon Dorje Chang. A happy Desi
Sangay secretly consulted the oracles to determine if the boy
born in *Monyul* was the true reincarnation. When his own
consultations proved auspicious, Desi ordered the child and his
mother to be transferred to Tsona under very strict secrecy.
Misunderstanding the purpose of Desi's order for strict secrecy, the Tsona officials kept the boy and the mother under
virtual house arrest for a long time.

In April 1697, the child reincarnation and mother were

secretly sent from Tsona to Nakartse under tight guard. At Nakartse, they were put up at the mansion of Yardok Khripon, an uncle of the Fifth Dalai Lama. In the same year, Nyimathang Shabdrung, a trusted minister of Desi Sangay Gyatso, was sent to the Manchu imperial court in Peking to make an official report of the demise of the Fifth Dalai Lama and the discovery of the Sixth to the K'ang Hsi emperor. In August of the same year, Desi's ministers announced the long concealed secret of the passing away of the Fifth and the discovery of the Sixth. Taken by surprise, grateful elder Tibetans thanked and prayed for the long life of the Desi, who, according to them, shouldered alone the burden of the demise of the Fifth Dalai Lama and did not let the people lament "the setting of the sun" but only rejoice "in its rising" now that the Sixth Dalai Lama had already been discovered. Only a few disgruntled officials complained that the secret had been concealed for so long. That a secret of such dimension could be kept for so long without letting the administration suffer any serious damage goes to prove the skill and drive of Desi Sangay. But the secret, once known to all the parties concerned, became the main cause and cornerstone of his downfall and Manchu infiltration.

In September 1697, Desi Sangay invited the Second Panchen Rinpoche Losang Yeshi to Nakartse. The young incarnation from *Monyul* received *getsul dompa* (novice monkhood vows) from the Panchen Rinpoche who gave the boy the spiritual name Losang Rigdzin Tsangyang Gyatso. After appointing a secretary, a chamberlain and other attendants befitting service to the high post of the Dalai Lama, the whole retinue left Nakartse. Reaching Nyethang after six days, Desi Sangay Gyatso with other state officials and abbots and monks of Sera, Gaden and Drepung—the three principal monasteries of Lhasa—offered *mendrel tensum* (Long Life Mandala) to Tsangyang Gyatso before a huge gathering of the local people. After the offering, Desi Sangay made a detailed report in front of the whole assembly, narrating the instruction of the Fifth Dalai Lama to conceal his demise to the discovery of the Sixth under extraordinary circumstances in *Monyul*. From Nyethang, Desi Sangay led the whole retinue to Lhasa, bringing joy to the hearts of the people to see their spiritual and temporal leader, the Sixth Dalai Lama, arrive at the Potala palace.

In October 1697, Tsangyang Gyatso was enthroned with grand ceremony as the Sixth Dalai Lama on the golden throne in the Potala palace, attended by the officials of the Government, monks from the three monasteries, Mongol princes, representatives of the K'ang Hsi emperor and the local people. Elaborate religious ceremonies, invoking prosperity, progress and peace in Tibet, were performed for days on end. Stupas were constructed in different parts of Tibet such as at Tsoka, Gyalthang, Dartsedo etc., and prayers were said in every monastery for the well-being of the new Dalai Lama and the country. With the enthronement finally over, a long period of spiritual training under the supervision of the Panchen Rinpoche, Desi Sangay himself and other selected teachers lay ahead for the young Dalai Lama.

Losang Rigdzin Tsangyang Gyatso, the newly discovered Sixth Dalai Lama, was born to a reputed Nyingma tantric family descended from the famed Terton (Treasure Text Finder) Pema Lingpa. A tall, handsome, talented and intelligent youth, his love of archery and the carefree outdoor life was stronger than for the strict training of a monastic surrounding. Though the learned Desi himself trained the young Dalai Lama in the religious and political world, and invited the Panchen Rinpoche and other selected lama scholars to tutor him, Tsangyang Gyatso's love for the outdoor life daily took him to the nearby parks and valleys in Lhasa, practising archery with his friends and enjoying the charms of nature. All the same, Tsangyang Gyatso was not a spoilt and arrogant youth. On the contrary, he was a simple man of austere personality who disdained pomp and show, preferred walking to riding horses and disliked large ceremonial retinues led by the grand chamberlain. Even in the Potala, he is said to have led a simple life without keeping any servants, making his own tea and sharing it with anyone who would come to receive his audience and blessings. When he was required to give discourses as part of his training he gave them in public places and parks in Lhasa, and not in the magnificent Potala or other grand monasteries. Though known for his carefree attitude towards his monastic training, Tsangyang Gyatso was given to intellectual pursuits and to the composing of learned treatises on various subjects. An excellent architect, he embellished and beautified the Norbu Lingka palace besides building the *lukhang* (Naga palace) at the back of the Potala, which became a prominent landmark of the Lhasa landscape. An enthusiastic dancer, he improved and modified many aspects of *cham*, the Tibetan monastic opera.

To Desi Sangay Gyatso and his associates, the young Dalai Lama turned out to be an enigma. Despite their best efforts to train him as a monk befitting the sacred position of the Dalai Lama, Tsangyang Gyatso turned out to be a carefree and apparently frivolous character who viewed his mentors' efforts, not with liking but with irritation and dislike. When the young Dalai Lama reached 20 years of age, the Desi requested him time and again to take the final initiation and consecration into monkhood—the *gelong* vows—and refrain from squandering his precious time in carefree wanderings day and night. The Desi even mentioned his plan to invite the Panchen Rinpoche from Tashi Lhunpo to bestow the *gelong* vows. But Desi Sangay's instructions fell on deaf ears as Tsangyang

16

Gyatso showed no enthusiasm whatsoever for the coming initiation into total monkhood.

In May 1702, Desi Sangay Gyatso, who could no longer bear the burden of Tsangyang Gyatso's irresponsibility, wrote a detailed and diplomatic letter to the Panchen Rinpoche, asking him for his revered intervention to persuade the young Dalai Lama to take his *gelong* vow, which he had delayed taking for so long under various pretexts. Getting wind of the Desi's letter to Panchen Rinpoche and perhaps in an effort to avoid the arrival of the Panchen Rinpoche in Lhasa at the Desi's secret invitation, Tsangyang Gyatso surprised the worried Desi with the news that he intended to journey to Tashi Lhunpo to receive the final initiation into monkhood. In great haste, Desi Sangay Gyatso arranged the journey. Accompanied by a number of important monk and lay officials, Tsangyang Gyatso left Lhasa for Tashi Lhunpo to meet his tutor Panchen Rinpoche.

The Desi's detailed letter and the rumours of Tsangyang Gyatso's behaviour had apparently worried the Panchen Rinpoche. When the latter was informed of Tsangyang Gyatso's journey to Tashi Lhunpo for the final consecration into monkhood, the Panchen Rinpoche, though ailing himself, travelled for some distance from Tashi Lhunpo to welcome his pupil and escort him to the monastery. But the young Dalai Lama did not proceed straight to Tashi Lhunpo monastery with his tutor; instead he took up residence in Zimkhang Gyaltsen Thonpo at Shigatse.

The Panchen Rinpoche, time and again, met Tsangyang Gyatso and earnestly tried to make the young Dalai Lama realise his plain duty "towards religion and living beings". In his effort to reform the adamant Tsangyang Gyatso, the Panchen Rinpoche was supported by a number of influential lamas and nobles sent by the Desi. This group or retinue included Demo and Sumpa incarnates, Taktse Shabdrung, Qosot Mongol prince Lhazang Khan (brother of Vangjal, the then Qosot "ruler" of Tibet) and the abbots of Sera, Gaden and Drepung.

As fate desired, a disappointment was in store for the Panchen Rinpoche, Desi Sangay Gyatso and the select members of the retinue. Though it is difficult to judge and state the precise intention of the young Dalai Lama in undertaking the journey to Shigatse, final initiation and consecration into monkhood do not seem to have been the main idea behind it. The young Dalai Lama appalled the Panchen Rinpoche and the retinue by revealing his intention to give up the novice monkhood vows which he had earlier received from the Panchen Rinpoche in 1697, instead of taking the final vows for which he had purposely made the journey. After prostrating thrice before the Panchen Rinpoche and begging forgiveness for not being able to fulfil the wishes of the honoured tutor, Tsangyang Gyatso renounced his *getsul* vows and returned to the state of layman. For a Tibetan born and brought up in an age of religious revival and near-total fanaticism, it must have called for an extraordinary amount of courage on the part of the young Tsangyang Gyatso to renounce his *getsul* vows before no less a personality than the Second Panchen Rinpoche, and deviate from the traditional practices followed by every Dalai Lama, before and since the Sixth. Yet his rejection of the monkhood vows did not amount to an abdication from the position of Dalai Lama. He maintained the temporal prerogatives of the Dalai Lama.

Bewildered and disturbed by this totally unexpected development, the abbots of the three monasteries, as well as Lhazang Khan and Desi Taktse approached the young Dalai Lama and pleaded with him not to renounce the *getsul* vows for the sake of the faith and country. But their appeals were to no avail. Tsangyang Gyatso remained firm in his decision not to resume the monkhood vows. In 1704, hearing that Tsangyang Gyatso was passing through Shigatse, Panchen Rinpoche invited him to visit Tashi Lhunpo once again, but Tsangyang Gyatso did not stop at Shigatse nor did he visit Tashi Lhunpo. He knew well that his revered tutor would plead with him to resume the monkhood vows forsaken by him two years before.

From the day he renounced his *getsul* vows, Tsangyang Gyatso dressed as a layman, mostly in light blue silk and brocades, kept his hair long and wore a number of striking rings on several fingers. Though he continued to live in the Potala, he often wandered to Lhasa, Valga, Chongyas and Gongkar, etc. Enjoying the newly gained freedom of a layman, he spent most of his time practising archery at the back of the Potala with his friends with whom, as dusk fell, he would visit Lhasa and Shol town, spending the nights in the taverns, drinking *chang* and singing love songs. Although the Lhasa and Shol wine shops were usually white in colour, some were later painted yellow. Popular belief has it that the yellow taverns were the consecrated abodes where Tsangyang Gyatso met his lovers during his nocturnal visits.

None was more disturbed and depressed by Tsangyang Gyatso's unusual behaviour than Desi Sangay, who had failed in his best efforts to train the young Dalai Lama. In his anger and desperation, Desi Sangay regarded bad company as the cause of the young Dalai Lama's degeneration. Added to the usual administrative burdens of a complex time, the Desi found that an increasing number of Mongols and Tibetan clergy questioned the behaviour of the young Dalai Lama and were beginning to show signs of wavering faith. On the one hand, the Desi instructed his associates not to question the behaviour of the young Dalai Lama, the incarnation of Avalokiteshvara; on the other hand, he intrigued and conspired with his associates Dapon Gachakpa, Darjungnas, Drungyig Tenzin and Apho Ngazom, to ambush and kill Drungkhor Thargyasnas—the closest friend of the Sixth Dalai Lama, whom they assumed arranged Tsangyang Gyatso's rendezvous with girls and was responsible for his degeneration and irresponsibility.

One night when Tsangyang Gyatso and his friends returned to the Potala, singing loudly after their nocturnal visits, the Desi's handpicked associates suddenly attacked them. Fortunately for Thargyasnas, earlier that evening, Tsangyang Gyatso had insisted that he himself change dress with the servant; and as a result Thargyasnas was dressed in Tsangyang Gyatso's attire while the servant wore Thargyasnas' clothes and Tsangyang Gyatso himself was dressed as the servant. In the sudden ambush and ensuing confusion, the servant was killed being mistaken for Thargyasnas. Realising their blunder, the ambushers attacked again and wounded Drungkhor Thargyasnas. The news of the incident spread like wildfire and the very next morning the whole of Lhasa was brimming with the incident. An enraged and beleaguered Tsangyang Gyatso consulted the *Lamo* oracle who revealed the identity of the assassins. Apho Ngazom was disgraced publicly by parading him around Lhasa city. The others involved were legally executed. Discovering the Desi's hand behind the plot, Tsangyang Gyatso remained aloof from and annoyed with the Desi, for whom he had lost much of his respect as he came to know the Desi from close quarters.

While Tsangyang Gyatso was rebelling against the rigid discipline and rigorous training forced upon him in his role as the highest incarnation of Tibet by renouncing his monkhood vows and taking a layman's lifestyle, the whole country was in the grip of a storm of power struggles and a whirlwind of political intrigues, resulting from the Desi's liaison with the restless Mongol chief Galden Khan of the Dzungar tribe and his estrangement with Lhazang Khan, who assumed full leadership of the Qosot Mongols after poisoning his brother Vangjal Khan in 1697. Tsangyang Gyatso's behaviour added further fuel to the already lit flame of the disastrous struggle. If, by concealing the death of the Fifth Dalai Lama, the Desi had succeeded in maintaining the allegiance of the faction-ridden Mongol tribes who fought the Manchu empire to regain the Tibetan territories lost in war, the Desi incurred their suspicion and wrath by revealing the secret he had guarded for 15 long years and by discovering a reincarnation who was unorthodox and outrageous in his role as the Sixth Dalai Lama.

By his dubious alliance with Galden Khan, the impatient chief of the Dzungar Mongols of Ili valley, the Desi had alerted the suspicions of the Manchu emperor of China who took a keen and renewed interest in Tibetan political affairs. Had Desi Sangay Gyatso followed the restraining policy of the Fifth Dalai Lama in his dealings with the various Mongol tribes, the K'ang Hsi emperor would not have been bothered. But by inculcating the friendship of the Dzungars, the Desi was aiding a potential rival of the Manchus, who viewed the rising power and kingdom of the Dzungars with concern and feared that the religious influence of the Dalai Lama might rally the whole of Mongolia, leading to their unification under Dzungar leadership, and threaten the very foundation of the Manchu empire. Therefore, it became necessary for the K'ang Hsi emperor to observe Tibetan political developments closely and bid for his chance to gain a strategic foothold in Tibet as soon as the opportunity offered itself.

For quite some time, the Mongol tribes around Kokonor were showing signs of increasing disunity. This was not missed by the K'ang Hsi emperor who, seeing the nascent disunity among the Mongols, took the chance to poison the ears of Mongol tribes like Chahar, Qosot, etc., against the Tibetan government of Desi Sangay Gyatso. The emperor showered titles and gifts on the Chahar tribes. He pointed out to the Qosot Desi Sangay's clandestine attempt to undermine Qosot influence by seeking Dzungar support. The emperor also accused the Desi of keeping the secret of the Fifth Dalai Lama's demise for so long merely as an excuse to prolong his personal power. Due to such effective Manchu infiltration and intrigue, the dominant Mongol tribes, viz. Chahar, Qosot and the Dzungars were soon completely divided among themselves. The Qosots, who helped the Fifth Dalai Lama to consolidate power and unify Tibet, now lost interest in safeguarding the Tibetan territories when they learnt that the Fifth Dalai Lama had already long since passed away.

Desi Sangay Gyatso was in a painfully difficult situation. The Sixth Dalai Lama had turned out to be the opposite of what he had hoped for, and he could no longer rule effectively in the latter's name. His rather unwise liaison with the Dzungars had estranged his relationship with the Qosot, whose chief Lhazang Khan was a man of energy and ruthless determination with the sole dream of reviving the defunct Qosot power in Tibet which his grandfather Gushri Khan had enjoyed. Forced by circumstances and also as a diplomatic move, the Desi resigned from active administration in 1703, and formally appointed his elder son Ngawang Rinchen to the regentship. This, however, was a political manoeuvre. In practice, complete power rested with the ex-Desi Sangay Gyatso whose relationship with Lhazang Khan further deteriorated. Sensing the mounting antagonism and rising strength of the Qosot, the ex-Desi attempted to fatally poison Lhazang Khan and his minister but they were saved from the effects of the poison by Jamyang Shepa of Drepung Gomang College. The latent power struggle flared up, and during the *Monlam* festival in 1705 Sangay Gyatso once again plotted to seize and assassinate Lhazang Khan. This plot could not be carried out as it was opposed, among others, by Jamyang Shepa and the abbots of the three monasteries, who reminded the ex-Desi of the kindness of Qosot Gushri Khan, grandfather of Lhazang, who had so courageously helped the Fifth Dalai Lama in consolidating his hold over the country.

The growing antagonism between the ex-Desi and Lhazang was creating a tense situation ripe for confrontation. As a device to save the country from the ravages of an imminent clash, the *Lamo* Oracle commanded Lhazang Khan to leave for Kokonor. Not being able to oppose the *Lamo's* command, Lhazang Khan started for Kokonor. Stopping on the banks of Nagchu for some time, he gathered his tribesmen and in 1705 marched back to Lhasa to confront the ex-Desi in a show of arms. Seeing the coming catastrophe, the abbots of the three monasteries interceded, and the Panchen Rinpoche personally wrote to Lhazang to refrain from the bloody confrontation. Lhazang did not issue a flat denial to the request of the Panchen Rinpoche and the abbots but expressed his desire to resume his march as far as Langdong, near Lhasa.

On the other hand, ex-Desi Sangay Gyatso flatly rejected any suggestion of a compromise and concentrated his forces from U-Tsang, Tod Ngari and Kham area in Lhasa. Instead of leading his troops to check Lhazang's advance on the capital, Sangay Gyatso kept his troops in Lhasa, waiting for Lhazang to advance unhindered. This was a mistake as the Tibetan troops were reduced to the disadvantage of fighting a defensive battle at best. This mistake proved to be fatal for the ex-Desi Sangay Gyatso.

On reaching Langdong, Lhazang divided his army into three columns. The Khan himself headed the left column advancing on Lhasa from the east, passing through Gamo-tren. The centre column was led by Tugus Jaisang, the Mongol commander who led his troops from the north of Lhasa, passing through Phenpo Gola. The right column was under Lhazang's wife Gyalmo Tsering Tashi, who planned to storm Lhasa from the west by way of the Tolung valley.

The decisive battle took place on the Go Pass where the ex-Desi's commander Dorje Rabten was killed by Mongol Jaisang. Soon afterwards, the ex-Desi was totally defeated with a loss of 400 men and had to accept the unconditional terms of the Qosot chief. Lhazang Khan took over the Lhasa administration and the ex-Desi journeyed to Gongkar Dzong in retirement. Unfortunately for the ex-Desi, Gyalmo Tsering Tashi harboured a personal grudge against him. At her command, Sangay Gyatso was captured on his way to Gongkar and beheaded on the 6th of September 1706 at Tolung Nangtse, the hill near the monastery of Kyomulung. Though Lhazang appeared to have no hand in the murder of the ex-Desi, it is said that Drungkhor Thargyasnas had secretly written to the Khan asking him to execute Sangay Gyatso. The Tibetans deeply regretted the tragic and ignominious way in which the ex-Desi was executed, since he was a most able administrator and accomplished scholar who shouldered the burden of Tibetan affairs for so long, but there was nothing that they could do under the superior strength of the Khan. Following the execution of the ex-Desi, his associates and supporters were closely watched. The regent Ngawang Rinchen was soon captured and later sent to China in the retinue of the Sixth Dalai Lama.

Lhazang Khan's successful defeat of Sangay Gyatso left him in full control of the administration. In this venture, he was supported by a number of prominent Tibetans. Among them was Miwang Pholanas Sonam Topgyal, a young Tibetan official who later played a significant role in Tibetan history. Now that the regent had been removed and Sangay Gyatso executed, Lhazang's next rival was the Sixth Dalai Lama himself. As the office of the Dalai Lama is a delicate institution, it naturally demanded extreme tact and skill to handle this operation, especially when the Sixth Dalai Lama had to be deposed from power right in front of Tibetan eyes. However, as later events showed, Lhazang completely failed to understand the Tibetan psychology and had misjudged the love and devotion which the Tibetans, both monk and lay, held for Tsangyang Gyatso.

As a first step towards the deposition of Tsangyang Gyatso, Lhazang Khan tried to gain the goodwill of the three principal monasteries by donating estates to them. He also tried to court the favour and support of the Panchen Rinpoche by sending his wife in 1705 to visit Tashi Lhunpo with rich gifts. Not only that, the Khan sought external support for his limited military power from the Manchu emperor K'ang Hsi who was only too willing to give both moral and military backing to the Qosot chief in order to keep in check the Dzungar Mongols.

Unfavourable reports, greatly exaggerating the activities of the Sixth Dalai Lama, were drawn up by Lhazang Khan and sent to the Manchu emperor. Soon both the emperor and Lhazang were getting impatient to depose the Dalai Lama. Yet not being certain of the Tibetan reaction to such a sacrilegious affront to their highest institution, Lhazang waited for an opportunity to offer itself. The K'ang Hsi emperor sent his Manchu lieutenant-colonel Hsi-chu to aid Lhazang in sending the Dalai Lama to China. Later, through the incarnate lama Chagney Dorjee of Koke-qoton, positive orders to arrest and send the Dalai Lama to China were released by the emperor. Fearing strong Tibetan resentment and reaction, Lhazang Khan could not depose the Dalai Lama straightaway. But being convinced of the necessity of removing the Dalai Lama for the consolidation of his own power, he called a meeting attended by the leading monastic officials and presided by Tri Rinpoche

Dhondup Gyatso. In this meeting, Lhazang announced that Tsangyang Gyatso should be deposed on the grounds that he was unworthy of his office. However, although Lhazang urged strongly, he failed to elicit an unanimous agreement to his plan from the Tibetan side. Nevertheless, Lhazang summoned Tsangyang Gyatso to his court and, reciting in detail his failings and vices, ordered him to leave for the Mongol military camp situated at Lhalu near Lhasa. He also despatched his soldiers to collect the personal belongings of the Sixth Dalai Lama from the Potala palace. The Tibetan people greatly resented this action and expressed their resentment by closing their shops and gathering in a large crowd around the Lhalu garden where the Dalai Lama was being kept under heavy guard by the Mongol troops. Led by the monks of the three monasteries, the large crowd pushed forward to have a glimpse of the Dalai Lama but were driven back by the troops who used arms on the protesting and panic-stricken people. On the 27th of June 1706, Lhazang declared the Dalai Lama deposed. The imperial envoy from China conveyed the emperor's summons to Tsangyang Gyatso. As the young Dalai Lama started on his last journey, he was followed by a large crowd of monks and lay people, who requested the Gaden Tri Rinpoche to lead them in their struggle to rescue the young Dalai Lama from Mongol-Manchu captivity. When, near Drepung, the crowds pressed too close, they were violently driven back by armed Qosot soldiers. In a desperate move, the angry and unarmed crowd attacked the escort with sticks and stones and succeeded in rescuing the Dalai Lama, whom they triumphantly brought back to his summer palace in Drepung monastery. The very next day, the monks consulted the *Nechung* oracle who declared Tsangyang Gyatso to be the true reincarnation of the Fifth Dalai Lama and added that "whoever would deny it, is beset with devilish delusions." The oracle's statement was greeted with joy and enthusiasm by the Tibetans, who became determined to defend the Dalai Lama to the last.

Angered by the strong Tibetan reaction against his infamous declaration and deposition of the Dalai Lama, Lhazang Khan sent his well-armed troops to Drepung the very next day and surrounded the monastery with artillery, preparing to set the aflame. A desperate resistance was put up by the unarmed monks led by the Tri Rinpoche, but it was of no avail before the trained and armed Qosot soldiers.

When the Dalai Lama saw that a massacre was bound to occur because of him, he stepped out of Drepung monastery with a few friends and advanced towards the Qosot troops. When his few friends fell fighting to the last, the Dalai Lama placed himself in the hands of the Qosot. Drepung, however, was sacked and looted for protecting the Dalai Lama. Tsangyang Gyatso was once again taken on his journey to China. When they reached Gunga-nor, a small lake to the south of Kokonor, Tsangyang Gyatso "disappeared". Written Chinese and Tibetan sources mention that he "died" of illness. But rumours of the time preserved by Desideri and other Italian missionaries in Lhasa presume that the Sixth Dalai Lama was "murdered".

After his unpopular act of deposing the Sixth Dalai Lama, Lhazang Khan committed an outrageous mistake that was to cost him his newly-won power. To the utter shock and dismay of the Tibetan people, Lhazang appointed a young monk, believed to be his natural son, as the "real" Sixth Dalai Lama. Even his mentor and co-conspirator, the K'ang Hsi emperor, delayed recognition of Lhazang's "Dalai Lama", knowing that the latter had gone too far in his game.

A few years later, the reincarnation of the Sixth Dalai Lama was discovered in Lithang as predicted in Tsangyang Gyatso's last song. Lhazang sent his men to search for him, but other Mongol tribes sympathetic to the Sixth Dalai Lama protected the Lithang child Kelsang Gyatso and shifted the family from Lithang to Derge. While the Manchu emperor was eagerly awaiting a chance to break through into Tibetan politics, the Dzungar Mongols, enraged by the murder of the regent Sangay and the deposing of the Sixth Dalai Lama, invaded the Qosots in Lhasa at the secret invitation of the three monasteries and defeated Lhazang Khan in 1717. In a heated hand-to-hand battle, Lhazang Khan killed 11 Dzungars before he himself was killed. Thus died the last Qosot ruler of Tibet. The Dzungar Mongols had gained the sympathy of the Tibetans for avenging Lhazang's execution of the regent Sangay Gyatso and also for deposing Lhazang Khan's "Dalai Lama". But they soon lost the sympathy and support of the people when they went around Lhasa in a wild frenzy of looting, raping and indiscriminately killing Nyingmapa lamas and destroying Nyingma and Bonpo monasteries throughout Central Tibet. Most importantly for the monks and people of Lhasa, the Dzungars had failed to bring the Seventh Dalai Lama from Lithang. The child Kelsang Gyatso, now under Manchu protection in Kubum monastery, had secretly been recognised as the real reincarnation of Tsangyang Gyatso after necessary tests by Tibetan officials secretly sent from Lhasa were judged as successful. It was at this critical juncture that the K'ang Hsi emperor, under the pretext of avenging Lhazang Khan's death and enthroning the Seventh Dalai Lama, sent his Manchu troops to Tibet. Defeated once, the emperor sent a stronger force. By then Tibetan resistance leaders like Kanchenas, the governor of western Tibet at Gartok and Pholanas of Tsang, who was deprived of his rank after the fall of Lhazang Khan, had already started reorganising resistance against the cruel Dzungars, who were finally overthrown by the combined might and tactics of the Manchu troops and Tibetan resistance in 1718.

The Manchu troops, by an extraordinary stroke of luck, got hold of the Lithang child Kelsang Gyatso, brought him to Lhasa and installed him on the throne at the Potala. Thus ended the Mongol supremacy in Tibet for good and the Manchu reign began which modern Chinese propaganda claims as the beginning of Chinese control in Tibet.

Historically, the Sixth Dalai Lama "died" or was "murdered" at Gunga-nor on 14th November 1706. But according to the *Secret Biography of the Sixth Dalai Lama*, his "disappearance" at Gunga-nor was the beginning of a very secret and curious spiritual adventure. After making secret pilgrimages to Central Tibet, Kham, India and Nepal, the Sixth Dalai Lama finally arrived at Alak-Shya, a far north region of Mongolia where he introduced the *Monlam Chenmo* (Great Prayer Festival) of Lhasa. The very next year, he secretly visited Peking. In 1724, he was said to have conducted the death rites in honour of the First Jetsum Dampa Ondur Gegen at Urga and established and consecrated the monastery of Jargud Thos-sam Dargyas Ling. If his years in Lhasa had been clouded with political intrigues, unrest and his own seemingly libertine way of life, the latter or the "secret" part of his life seems equally devoted to the propagation of Buddhism in Mongolia. According to this version, Tsangyang Gyatso passed away in 1746, 40 years after his "disappearance" from Gunga-nor lake.

It is of significance to note here that on the life and the "secret life" of the Sixth Dalai Lama, the Thirteenth Dalai Lama told Sir Charles Bell: "He (the Sixth Dalai Lama) did not observe even the rules of a fully ordained priest. He drank wine habitually. And he used to have his body in several places at the same time, e.g. in Lhasa, in Kongpo and elsewhere. Even the place where he retired to the Honourable Field (Death) is uncertain: one tomb of his is in Alasher in Mongolia, while there is another in the Rice-Heap (Drepung) monastery. Showing many bodies at the same time is disallowed in all the sects of our religion, because it causes confusion in the work.

"One of his bodies used to appear in the crowd in the Reception Hall of the Seventh Dalai Lama. One is said to appear also at my receptions, but I am unable to say whether this is true or not."

Whether Tsangyang Gyatso is the true reincarnation of the Fifth Dalai Lama was a question decided for the Tibetans of his time by the *Nechung* Oracle whom the monks and the people consulted before his final arrest by Lhazang's troops in 1706. Because of Lhazang's defamatory reports regarding the behaviour of Tsangyang Gyatso, the Manchu emperor was said to have sent his own wise men to examine Tsangyang Gyatso. After a prolonged and careful examination, the emperor's wise men reportedly declared that the youth manifested all the wondrous signs of a bodhisattva.

Legend has it that Desi Sangay Gyatso, while praying for the speedy reincarnation of the departing Fifth Dalai Lama, reqested him to make the Dalai Lama institution hereditary in order to save the country from the unnecessary administrative wastage and complications created by the interregnum of the Dalai Lama's demise and his rediscovery, during which regents usually rule. The Fifth Dalai Lama, according to the legend, is said to have assented to this request and instructed the Desi that his reincarnation should be allowed full freedom to behave as he desired, without any objections or obstruction. References to a sweetheart born in the valley of Chungyal are found in several songs of the Sixth Dalai Lama. Tibetans widely believe that had Tsangyang Gyatso met his sweetheart from Chungyal, the son would have made the Dalai Lama institution hereditary and Tibet would have become invincible to any foreign power. But, it is said, due to the general deterioration of Tibet's collective virtue, Tsangyang Gyatso never met the sweetheart from Chungyal. Whatever the basis of this legend, Desi Sangay Gyatso did not keep his promise of letting the Sixth Dalai Lama do as he wanted since it was the Desi who subjected him to the monastic training against which Tsangyang Gyatso had rebelled with such dogged determination. Another interesting fact is that although the Sixth Dalai Lama abandoned his monastic training and gave up his monkhood vows, he never rejected the temporal office of the Dalai Lama and continued to reside in the Potala palace. After all, there is no hard and fast rule that a Dalai Lama must think and behave in a particular way. The choice is left to the Dalai Lama himself and Tsangyang Gyatso chose a less common path.

Possibly Desi Sangay's own dissolute lifestyle and love for the mundane and sensual pleasures of soft music and beautiful women were responsible for the twists and turns of Tsangyang's life. It was common knowledge in Lhasa of that time that no beautiful lady was safe from the Desi's sight, and that he later let his mistresses interfere in the administration of the country. The Desi's loose ways cost him his most trusted friends, who deserted him when he did not reform at their repeated requests. A song attributed to Tsangyang Gyatso reads:

> Do not tell me
> 'Tsangyang! You are dissolute,'
> Just as you desire pleasure
> I, too, desire pleasure and comfort.

Here he seems to be addressing the Desi who, despite his own poor behaviour, was trying to correct Tsangyang Gyatso.

Tibetan scholars give Tsangyang's affairs with his sweethearts a tantric light and raise them above the usual affairs of ordinary human beings. Many scholars, both Western and Tibetan, attribute a secondary, tantric meaning to his mundane activities. Some claim him to be the centre of a secret Nyingma tantric cult which indulged in dubious tantric sexual practices. Be that as it may, it goes without saying that Tsangyang Gyatso was unique not only among the Dalai Lamas but also among most of the spiritual leaders of world history, in that his ambiguous behaviour did not destroy the faith of the Tibetans who continued to love him dearly and worship him with stainless faith. Since Tsangyang Gyatso was born and brought up in a Nyingma family advanced in tantric practices, it was perhaps unwise on the part of Desi Sangay Gyatso to force the strict Gelug training on the young Tsangyang, who proved to be an uncomfortable and controversial blend of the two.

Whatever controversy later historians see in his life and times and whatever doubts later generations cast on the Sixth Dalai Lama, the depth of Tibetan love and faith came to the fore when the Manchu emperor declared the Lithang child Kelsang Gyatso not as the Seventh but as the Sixth Dalai Lama, thereby implying his rejection of Tsangyang Gyatso as a true reincarnation. The Tibetans gallantly ignored the emperor's order by addressing Kelsang Gyatso, who fulfilled the prophecy of Tsangyang's last son by "returning from Lithang", as the Seventh and not as the Sixth in his line.

Leaving aside the unfortunate politics that surrounded his desolate life, Tsangyang Gyatso, the "Ocean of Melodious Songs", brought to holy Lhasa some of the purest and most beautiful lyrics of all time. Great as a lover of wine and women; melodious as a singer of timeless love songs and equally tragic as a national hero having the status of a Dalai Lama, the highest incarnation of Central Asia reduced to a heroic pawn in the hands of the Qosot Lhazang Khan, Tsangyang Gyatso became a legend within his short lifespan. Living as the source and centre of power in a power-hungry time, Tsangyang led an insecure and desolate life in constant fear of the scheming Lhasa court. The justice which he did not attain in his lifetime, he hoped to achieve in his death. One of his songs says:

> *Yama*, the mirror of my *karma*
> Residing in the realm of death,
> You must judge and grant justice.
> For, while alive, I had no justice.

Like all the Dalai Lamas, the Sixth was an extraordinary incarnation. Much evidence still remains of his many miraculous deeds and performances. While still a child in *Mon* (Tawang), he is said to have magically left his footprints on stone and to have inscribed mystic writings on the rocks with his bare fingers. Visitors today can still see these footprints and writings in Tawang, attributed to him.

Of exceptional interest is the tale of the three sandalwood trees Tsangyang Gyatso planted close to each other before leaving Tawang. He prophesied that the three trees would grow identical to each other on the day he would once again visit Tawang. In the year 1959 the local people noticed to their amazement that the three sandalwood trees were growing equal to each other in size and had become identical in shape. Unfortunately, the trees caught fire which plunged the local people into anxiety and dismay. Soon afterwards they heard of the unrest in Tibet caused by the Chinese invasion, and after a week-long spectacle of crowds of foreign and Indian pressmen, security personnel and unusual suspense, they saw that the Dalai Lama had indeed come to Tawang once again, this time as the Great Fourteenth, on his way to exile in India.

Tsangyang Gyatso
The Poet of the People

Losang Rigdzin Tsangyang Gyatso, whose name means the "Precious Ocean of Pure Melody" was one of the most extraordinary poets that Tibet ever produced. He and the great Yogi Milarepa are the two most original and popular poets of Tibet's history. Their poetry, free from the flowery metaphors of the classical school and rigid didacticism of traditional Tibetan verse, found universal appeal throughout the country, all through the centuries to follow. Basically, both were singers: they sang spontaneous songs of their experiences. Neither of them wrote down their songs expecting that later generations would read them. They simply sang as and when they were inspired. The poetry is in the spontaneity and direct simplicity of these rich songs. Radically different from each other in style and content, the poetry and the songs of these two original poets of Tibet have drawn their initial inspiration from folk traditions and improved and enriched the tradition to such an extent that, due to their influence, folk poetry eventually attained a permanent place in Tibetan literature.

Described by H.E. Richardson as "a poet of the most unusual kind...the only writer of lyrical verse that Tibet has produced", and by Luciano Petech as "one of the finest poets of Tibet, nay, the only erotic poet of the country", the Sixth Dalai Lama was essentially a poet of the people, a poet whose songs have found a special and permanent place in the hearts of common Tibetans, especially in the young whose joy of love, despair of loneliness and frustration with social injustice so often were reflected in his songs. L.S. Savitsky, the well-known Russian Tibetologist, points out that Tsangyang Gyatso's verses are "often filled with a sentiment of social protest against the feudal order which obstructed the happiness of the common people". Sixth in the line of the Dalai Lamas, Tsangyang Gyatso was the first Dalai Lama to write lyrical verses and popularise lyric poetry in Tibet.

Written in simple, clear and expressive language, the verses were restrained in tone and economic and accurate in their use of epithets and similes. Almost shorn of literary devices, the verses nonetheless excel in their rare description of the basic human emotions and experiences of love, loyalty, loneliness and betrayal etc., with the use of a wide range of native images. Though these verses have been widely referred to as erotic love songs, and since their creation have been sung in every part of Tibet at festivals and other social occasions, not all the songs are inspired by love or eroticism. Although the sentiment of love plays an important and dominant part in these songs, even when a song has love as the theme it is not often the joys of love but rather the despair and bitterness of love lost through betrayal or the longing for the joys of love yet to be, that are most often expressed.

In a sense, the songs of Tsangyang Gyatso have been no less controversial than the man himself. Because it was a Dalai Lama who sang these pure songs of love and life, Tibetans attach a special significance to them. Had they come from anybody less than a Dalai Lama, they would have been forgotten long ago, for it did not need the special genius of a Dalai Lama to compose these songs. But what has made these delightful songs timeless and universally appealing is the fact that they reflect the psychic state of the young and desolate Tsangyang Gyatso who unwillingly became the focus and pawn of a turbulent crisis during one of the most power-hungry periods in the history of Tibet.

Most Tibetan scholars have exalted the relationship of Tsangyang Gyatso with his sweethearts above the usual human behaviour, and spread the common belief that his songs contain hidden tantric meanings lost to the ordinary reader. That the

Sixth Dalai Lama was advanced both in the theory and practice of tantra is established beyond doubt by his tantric treatises. Besides, most of his songs seem to contain more than what they say. Many of them contain sharp social satire and anger against social injustice, while others make mockery of the monks who are not true to their vows and still others deal with the difficult choice between a religious retreat and the warm embrace of a sweetheart. But it is beyond the present translator to establish positively that all the songs of the Sixth Dalai Lama contain secret tantric meanings. It may be more correct and safer to state that some of the verses indirectly show his deep knowledge and practise of tantra, as is clear from the one song in which he has claimed:

> Never have I slept without a sweetheart
> Nor have I spent a single drop of sperm.

This claim of control over his flow of sperm openly declared his grasp and mastery of tantric practices. But the interpretations of his songs will differ. Some will take them for love songs while others will insist on more profound meanings. In this lies part of the charm and appeal of the songs. But as in all profound poetry, each reader is moved by his or her own personal experience of it. Tsangyang Gyatso's songs undoubtedly inspire his readers with different levels of spiritual and mundane meanings, and thus perhaps will bring a new message to different generations of lovers of songs and poetry.

Despite the difficulty of translating both the meaning and the poetry of the songs, two complete translations already exist in the English language: *The Love Songs of the Sixth Dalai Lama*, translated both into Chinese and English by Yu Dawachuan, published in Taipei in 1939; and *Love Songs and Proverbs of Tibet* by Marion H. Duncan, published in New York in 1959, which includes the "Love Songs of the Sixth Dalai Lama" in its Chapter VI. In his *The Blue Winged Bee*, published first in

1969 by Anvil Press Poetry, U.K., Peter Whigham has done an interpretative translation of 30 songs of the Sixth Dalai Lama. More recently, a new translation of the songs entitled *Wings of the White Crane* by Gary Houston has been published in the USA, with an intriguing introduction by Helmut Hoffman.

In addition, many works on Tibetan history and culture have several original translations from the songs in their sections on the Sixth Dalai Lama or on folk literature, etc. Mention must be made of the delightful translations of some of the songs by Sir Charles Bell in his *Tibet: Past and Present* (Oxford, 1924) and *The Portrait of the Dalai Lama* (Collins, 1946). Bell's translations have to a great extent captured both the meaning and poetry of the songs, although unfortunately only of a few songs from the whole collection are included.

Thubten Jigme Norbu and Collin Turnbull's *Tibet* (Penguin, 1976) contains several original translations of the songs. Moreover, their entire Chapter XIV entitled "A Riddle of Love" is an attempt to unravel the riddle that is Tsangyang Gyatso. Therefore, most of their translations differ radically from translations done by others. Strong efforts to bring out the hidden meaning of the songs by Thubten Jigme Norbu can clearly be gleaned. For example, Richardson and Snellgrove's translation:

> I went to seek instruction
> At the feet of my worthy lama;
> But my thoughts could not be kept
> They escaped to my beloved.

in *A Cultural History of Tibet* (Weidenfeld and Nicholson, London, 1968) becomes in Norbu and Turnbull's translation:

> I went to my teacher, with devotion filled
> To learn of the Lord Buddha.
> My teacher taught, but what he said escaped;
> For my mind was full of compassion,

Full of that Compassionate One who loves me,
She has stolen my mind.

Marion H. Duncan's

Mt. Sumeru the golden central mountain
Must be unswerving and remaining steadfast;
So that the outer revolving sun and moon,
Will not be contemplating going astray.

become in Norbu and Turnbull's translation:

My Compassionate One, be like the holy
mountain, Rirab Lhunpo.
Stay still and let the sun and moon encircle you,
Day and night,
Faithful, like the sun and moon,
Shall I be to you.

Besides these translations in which the "secret" meaning
of the songs is "revealed" by bringing to the fore the concept
of the Compassionate One etc., Norbu and Turnbull's translations contain some of the most poetic renderings so far. To
quote one example:

To say farewell
Is to be sad
Be not sad, my love,
For after every parting
Comes another meeting.

Finally, the number of songs attributed to the Sixth Dalai
Lama differ. There are 54, 62 or even more, according to
different editions. While most have taken the song:

In my Palace, the place of Heaven on Earth
They call me Rigdzin Tsangyang Gyatso

38

Chenresig Reincarnate
But, below my Palace,
In the little town of Shol,
They call me Chebo Tangsang Wangpo, the
    Profligate,
For my Lovers are many.
(*Tibet*: Norbu and Turnbull)

to have been sung by the Sixth Dalai Lama himself, the recognised Tibetan historian T.W. Shakabpa writes in *Tibet: A Political History* (Yale University Press, 1967), that "the courtesans of Lhasa began to sing a song about the Sixth Dalai Lama:

In the Potala, he is Rinchen Tsangyang Gyatso
But, in Lhasa and Shol, he is a gay young blade

clearly denying that the song may be attributed to Tsangyang Gyatso.

The present translation of the *Songs of the Sixth Dalai Lama* is not intended to be read as an improvement upon the many translations of the songs that already exist in the English language. The sole aim and purpose of the present translation is to present the readers with what young Tibetans brought up in exile find in our ancestral history and culture. If only a glimpse of the Tibet of yesteryear appears through the pages of this translation and if only a fraction of the nostalgia and inspiration that swells in young Tibetans today in their cultural and literary heritage comes through to the readers, my purpose and aim of translating these sweet and sad songs are amply served.

K. Dhondup
Dharamsala
1981.

༄༅།། པ་རྒྱལ་བ་ཚངས་དབྱངས་རྒྱ་མཚོའི་
མགུལ་གླུ་བཞུགས་སོ།།

Songs of the
Sixth Dalai Lama
Tsangyang Gyatso

གཞར་ཕྱུགས་རེ་བོའི་ཙེ་ནས། །

དགར་གསལ་རྣྭ་བ་གཞར་བྱུང་། །

མ་སྨྲེས་ཨ་མའི་ཞལ་རས། །

ཡིད་ལ་འཁོར་འཁོར་བྱས་བྱུང་། །

ནཉིང་བཏབ་པའི་ལྗང་གཞོན། །

ད་ལོ་སོག་མའི་ཕོན་ཕྱུག །

ཕོ་གཞོན་རྒས་པའི་ལུས་པོ། །

ཙྀ་གཞུ་རེ་ལས་གྱིང་བ། །

1

Over the eastern hill rises

The smiling face of the moon;

In my mind forms

The smiling face of my beloved.

2

Yesterday's young sprouting shoots

Are withered straws today,

Like the ageing body of a youth

Stiff bent as a southern bow.

རང་སེམས་སྡིང་བའི་མི་དེ། །

གདན་གྱི་མདུན་མར་བྱུང་ན། །

རྒྱ་མཚོའི་གཏིང་ནས་ནོར་བུ། །

ཡོན་པ་དེ་དང་མཉམ་བྱུང༌། །

འགྲོ་ཞོར་ལམ་བུའི་སྐྱིད་ཕྲུག །

ཡུས་དེ་ཞིམ་པའི་བུ་མོ། །

གཡུ་ཆུང་གྱུ་དཀར་བརྗེད་ནས། །

རྐྱུར་བ་དེ་དང་འདྲ་བྱུང༌། །

3

If only I could wed

The one whom I love,

Joys of gaining the choicest gem

From the ocean's deepest bed would be
mine.

4

She smells sweet of body

My sweetheart, the highway queen;

Like the worthless white turquoise

She was found, to be thrown away.

མི་ཆེན་དཔོན་པོའི་སྲས་མོ། །

ཁམས་འབྲས་མཆར་ལ་བསྐུས་ན། །

ཁམ་སྟོང་མཐོན་པོའི་རྩེ་ནས། །

འབྲས་བུ་སྨིན་པ་འདྲ་བྱུང་། །

སེམས་པ་ཕར་ལ་ཕྱིར་ནས། །

མཆན་མོའི་གཉིད་ཐེབས་གཅོག་གིས། །

ཉིན་མོ་ལག་ཏུ་མ་ལོན། །

ཡིད་ཐང་ཆད་རོགས་ཡིན་པ། །

5

Longing for the landlord's daughter

Blossoming in youthful beauty

Is like pining for peaches

Ripening on the high peach trees.

6

Sleepless I am

Because I am in love;

Fatigue and frustration overwhelm

When day brings not my beloved to
  me.

མེ་ཏོག་ནམ་ཟླ་ཡལ་སོང་། །

གཡུ་སྦྲང་སེམས་པ་མ་སྐྱོ། །

བྱམས་པ་ལས་འཕྲོ་ཟད་པས། །

ད་ནི་སྐྱོ་ཀྱུ་མི་འདུག །

ༀ

ཅེ་ཐོག་པ་མོའི་ཁ་ལ། །

སྐྱི་སེར་རྐྱང་གི་ཕོ་ག །

མེ་ཏོག་སྦྲང་བུ་གཉིས་ཀྱི། །

འབྲལ་མཚམས་བྱེད་མཁན་ལོས་ཡིན།།

Spring flowers fade in the fall;

It is not for the turquoise bees to mourn.

I and my sweetheart are fated to part;

It is not for us to cry.

Frost gathers on the glistening flowers

And then the cold north wind blows.

The frost and the wind must have come

To drive the bees away from the flowers.

དང་པ་མཚོ་ལ་ཆགས་ནས། །

རེ་ཞིག་སྡུད་དགོས་བསམས་ཀྱང་། །

མཚོ་མོ་དར་ཁ་བརྐྱིགས་ནས། །

རང་སེམས་ཁོ་ཐག་ཆོད་སོང་། །

གྲུ་གུན་སེམས་པ་མེད་ཀྱང་། །

ཏ་མགོས་ཕྱི་མིག་བལྟས་བྱུང་། །

ཁྲེལ་གཡུང་མེད་པའི་བྲམས་པས། །

ང་ལ་ཕྱི་མིག་མི་ལྟ། །

In love with the lake,

The swan longs to stay longer,

But the ice covers the lake

And the swan flies

With no regrets.

The wooden horse, though devoid of
feeling,

Glances back from the ferry;

But my beloved, devoid of gratitude,

Does not even glance at me.

ཆུང་འདྲིས་བྱམས་པའི་རྐྱང་བསྐྱེད། །

ལྷུང་མའི་ལོགས་ལ་བཅུགས་ཡོད། །

ལྷུང་སྲུང་ཨ་རྫོ་ཞལ་རོས། །

རྫོ་ག་རྒྱབ་པ་མ་གནང་། །

ཕྲིས་པའི་ཡི་གེ་ནག་ཆུང་། །

ཆུ་དང་ཐིག་གས་པས་འཇིག་སོང་། །

མ་ཕྲིས་སེམས་ཀྱི་རི་མོ། །

བསུབས་ཀྱང་ཟུབ་རྒྱུ་མི་འདུག །

I have hoisted prayer-flags

For the good luck of my beloved.

Forest keeper, Ajo Shelngo,

Do not trample her good luck flags.

Drops of rain wash away

The love songs written in

Black and white

But love, though unwritten,

Remains long after, in the heart.

རྒྱབ་པའི་ནག་རྐྱང་ཐེ་ཚུས། །

གསུང་སྐད་འགྱུར་ནི་མི་ཤེས། །

ཁྱལ་དང་གཞུང་གི་ཐེའུ། །

སོ་སོའི་སེམས་ལ་སྐྱོན་དང་། །

སྟོང་ལྷུན་དུ་ལྱོའི་མེ་ཏོག །

མཆོད་པའི་རྫས་ལ་ཡེབས་ན། །

གཡུ་སྦྲང་གཞོན་ཉུ་ང་ཡང་། །

ལྕ་ཁང་ནང་ལ་ཁྲིད་དང་། །

13

The legal seal to seal documents

Cannot utter a word in witness;

Better it is to seal one's heart

With the seal of truth and justice.

14

If the blossoming hollyhock is leaving

As an offering to the altar,

Leave not the young turquoise bee behind:

"Take me with you,

To the altar."

སེམས་སོང་བུ་མོ་མི་བཞུགས། །

དམ་པའི་ཆོས་ལ་ཕེབས་ན། །

ཕོ་གཞོན་ང་ཡང་མི་སྡོད། །

རི་ཁྲོད་འགྲིམ་ལ་ཐལ་འགྲོ། །

མཚན་ལྡན་བླ་མའི་དྲུང་དུ། །

སེམས་འཁྲིད་ཞུ་བར་ཕྱིན་པས། །

སེམས་པ་འགྲོར་ཡང་མི་ཐུབ། །

བྱམས་པའི་ཕྱོགས་ལ་འཁོར་སོང་། །

If my beloved who stole my heart

Renounces the world for the holy
   dharma,

My youth too shall seek

Retreat in a hermitage.

I incline myself

To the teachings of my lama

But my heart secretly escapes

To the thoughts of my sweetheart.

བསྐྱམས་པའི་བླ་མའི་ཞལ་རས། །

ཡིད་ལ་འཁར་རྒྱུ་མི་འདུག །

མ་བསྐྱམས་བྱམས་པའི་ཞལ་རས། །

ཡིད་ལ་ཡང་ཡང་ཤར་བྱུང༌། །

སེམས་པ་འདི་ལ་འགྲོ་འགྲོ། །

དམ་པའི་ཆོས་ལ་ཕྱིན་ན། །

ཚེ་གཅིག་ལུས་གཅིག་ཉིད་ལ། །

སངས་རྒྱས་ཐོབ་པ་འདུག་གོ །

Even if meditated upon,

The face of my lama comes not to me,

But again and again comes to me

The smiling face of my beloved.

If I could meditate upon the *dharma*

As intensely as I muse on my beloved

I would certainly attain enlightenment

Surely, in this one lifetime.

དགའ་བ་ཤེལ་རི་གནས་རྒྱུ། །

ཀླུ་བདུད་རྡོ་རྗེའི་ཞིལ་པ། །

བདུད་ཙེ་སྨན་གྱི་ཕབ་རྒྱུན། །

ཆང་མ་ཨེ་ཤེས་མཁའ་འགྲོ། །

དམ་ཚིག་གཅང་མས་བདུང་ན། །

ངན་སོང་མྱོང་དགོས་མི་འདུག །

ཀྲུང་རྟ་ཡར་འགྲོའི་དུས་ལ། །

ཀྲུང་བསྐྱེད་དར་ལྱོག་བཅུགས་པས། །

མཇངས་མ་མ་བཟང་བུ་མོའི། །

མགྲོན་པོ་ལ་ནི་ཕོས་བྱུང་། །

The snow pure water of the holy *Dagpa
    Shelrill**

The dew drops of the rare *Naga-Vajra
    grass*

Essence of the ambrosia

Fermented into wine by *Yeshi Khandro*

Incarnated as a wine-maiden

Saves the drinkers from rebirth in the
    lower realms,

If the ambrosia wine is drunk with the
    right mental attitude.

20

When my luck was good

I hoisted auspicious prayer-flags

And the young lady of noble birth

Hosted me at her home.

---

*This is an inadequate translation of this highly complex song. According to
Tibetan scholars, this song is purely tantric and partially reveals Tsangyang
Gyatsho's mastery over tantra.

སོ་དཀར་པགས་པའི་འདུམ་མདངས། །

འཆུགས་གྲུལ་སྟི་ལ་བསྐུས་ནས། །

མིག་ཟུར་ཕྱུ་མོའི་སྐྱིལ་མཆམས། །

གཞིན་པའི་གདོང་ལ་བསྐུས་བྱུང་། །

དེ་ཚང་སེམས་ལ་སོང་ནས། །

འགྲོགས་འདྲིས་ཨེ་ཡོང་རྗིས་པས། །

འཆེ་བྱལ་བྱེད་ན་མིན་པ། །

གསོན་བྱལ་མི་བྱེད་གསུངས་བྱུང་། །

She sparkled her smile

To the crowd in the tavern,

But from the corner of her eyes

She spoke of her love to me.

So enchanted by her

I enquired if she would be mine.

"Only death can part us,"

She said;

"In this life, nothing can

Separate us."

མཇོངས་མའི་ཕྱུགས་དང་བསྲུན་ན། །

ཅེ་འདིའི་ཚོས་སྐལ་ཆད་འགྲོ། །

དབེན་པའི་རི་ཁྲོད་འགྲིམས་ན། །

བུ་མོའི་ཕྱུགས་དང་འཁལ་འགྲོ། །

འཇུམ་དང་སོ་དཀར་སྟོན་ཕྱོགས། །

གཟིན་པའི་རྫོ་བྲིད་ཡིན་འདུག །

སྐྱིང་ནས་ཀ་ཆ་ཡོད་མེད། །

དབུ་མནའ་བཤེས་རྒྱགས་གནང་དང་། །

64

Accepting the desires of my darling
  will despair

My only chance to bow before the
  dharma,

Yet my retreat into solitary hermitage

Will break my beloved's tender heart.

Your sweet smile is

To steal away my young heart.

If your love for me is true,

Promise me so

From the depths of your heart.

སྐྱིད་ཐུབ་ཡིད་འཕྲོག་ཤྭ་མོ། །

རྫོན་བ་རང་གིས་ཞེན་ཀྱང་། །

དབང་ཆེན་མི་ཡི་དཔོན་པོ། །

ནོར་བཟང་རྒྱལ་བུས་འཕྲོགས་སོང་། །

ནོར་བུ་རང་ལ་ཡོད་དུས། །

ནོར་བུའི་ནོར་ཉམས་མ་ཚོང་། །

ནོར་བུ་མི་ལ་ཤོར་དུས། །

སྐྱིད་ཆུང་སྐྱོད་ལ་ཆངས་བྱུང་། །

I, a hunter, captured

Yitrog Lhamo, the enchanting fairy;

But *Norzang Gyalu*, the mighty lord of
  men,

Snatched her away from me.

When the gem was mine

I cared not, and ignored its value.

Now that the gem is lost to others,

Melancholy overwhelms me

As its pure worth dawns on me.

རང་ལ་དགའ་བའི་བྱམས་པ། །

གཞན་གྱི་མདུན་མར་ལྷུངས་སོང་། །

ཁོང་ནང་སེམས་པའི་གཅོང་གི། །

ཡུས་པོའི་ག་ཡང་བསྐྱམས་སོང་། །

སྐྱིང་སྡུག་ཀྱུ་ལ་ཤོར་སོང་། །

མོ་ཕྱུ་ཉིས་འབུལ་རན་སོང་། །

བུ་མོ་དུང་སེམས་ཅན་མ། །

ཀྲི་ལམ་ནང་ལ་འཁོར་སོང་། །

27

My sweetheart who truly loved me

Has been stolen to wed another.

I am sick with longing sorrow

And frustration emaciates my frail body.

28

In my dreams often

I see my lost beloved;

A soothsayer I must seek

To search for her soon for me.

བུ་མོར་འཆི་བ་མེད་ན། །

ཆང་ལ་འཇུད་པ་མི་འདུག །

གཞིན་པའི་གཏད་ཀྱི་སྐྱབས་གནས། །

འདི་ལ་བཅོལ་བས་ལོས་ཆོག །

བུ་མོ་ཨ་མར་མ་སྐྱེས། །

ཁམ་བུའི་ཤིང་ལས་སྐྱེས་སམ། །

ཨ་གསར་ཟད་པ་ཁམ་བུའི། །

མེ་ཏོག་དེ་ལས་མགྱོགས་པ། །

If the maiden will live forever

The wine will flow evermore.

The tavern is my haven;

With wine I am content.

Was the girl born of a human mother

Or from the stem of a peach tree?

Her love blooms and as soon withers

As the fast blossoms of spring peaches.

བུ་མོ་ཆུང་འདྲིས་བྱམས་པ། །
སྡུང་ཀིའི་རེ་གས་བཅུད་མིན་ནམ། །
ཤ་འདྲིས་པགས་འདྲིས་བྱུང་ཡང་། །
རེ་ལ་ཡར་གྲབས་མཛད་ཀྱི། །

ཏ་གོད་རེ་ཡར་རྒྱབ་པ། །
རྩེ་དང་ཞག་ས་པས་ཟིན་ཀྱི། །
བྱམས་པ་དོ་ལོག་རྒྱབ་པ། །
ཐུགས་དོ་ཟིན་པ་མི་འདུག །

72

My beloved from childhood

Seems to be of the wolf's race;

Even after many nights together

She tries to escape,

Like the wolves, to the hills.

Traps and lassoes can capture

Wild horses fleeing over the hills;

But nothing, not even magic, can charm

The rebel-beloved, who has ceased to
    love her lover.

བྲག་དང་རྐྱང་པོ་བཟེབས་ནས། །

ཀྲོད་པོའི་སྐྲོ་ལ་གནེན་བྱུང་། །

གཡོ་ཅན་རྟ་བག་ཅན་གྱིས། །

ང་ལ་གཉན་པོ་བྱུས་བྱུང་། །

སྦྱིན་པ་ཁ་མེར་གཏིང་ནག །

སད་དང་སེ་རའི་གཞི་མ། །

བན་དེ་སྐྱུ་མིན་སེར་མིན། །

སངས་རྒྱས་བསྐྲུན་པའི་དགྲ་པོ། །

To the wings of this eagle

The wind and the rocks have been cruel.

The sly and scheming ones

Have harassed me, always without ceas-
ing.

Pink clouds

Hide frost and hailstorms;

He who is a half-monk

Is a hidden enemy of the *dharma*.

ས་རེ་ལ་ཞུ་གཏིང་འཁྱགས་རེ་བ། །

རྟ་ཕོ་གཏིང་ས་མ་རེད། །

གསར་འགྲོགས་བྱམས་པའི་ཕྱོགས་སུ། །

སྙིང་གཏམ་ཤོད་ས་མ་རེད། །

ཆོས་ཆེན་བཙོ་ལྡའི་སྨྲ་བ། །

ཡིན་པ་འདྲ་བ་འདུག་སྟེ། །

སྨྲ་བའི་དཀྱིལ་གྱི་རེ་ཕོད། །

ཆོ་ཟད་ཆར་ཉི་འདུག་གོ །

Over the slippery surface of the frozen
  depth

Let not your stallion trot;

Towards the charms of a new-found
  lover

Let not your secrets scatter.

The moon tonight seems

To be the full moon,

But the hare* inside the moon

Does not seem to be alive.

*Refers to a popular Tibetan belief that a giant hare resides in the moon.

ལྟ་བ་འདི་ཉམས་ཐར་འགྲོ། །

ཏིང་མའི་ལྟ་བ་ཆུར་ཡོད། །

བཀྲ་ཤིས་ལྟ་བ་དཀར་པོ། །

ལྟ་སྟོད་ཕྱུགས་ལ་མཇལ་ཡོད། །

དབུས་ཀྱི་རི་རྒྱལ་ལྷུན་པོ། །

མི་འགྱུར་བརྟན་པར་བཞུགས་དང་། །

ཉི་མ་ལྟ་བའི་བསྐོར་ཕྱོགས། །

ནོར་ཡོང་བསམ་པ་མི་འདུག །

The moon goes away this month,

Next month the moon will rise.

My beloved and I shall meet

When next month the moon rises anew.

Rirab Lhunpo, the central mountain of
  the Universe,

Stand steadfast and unswerving.

The sun and the moon shall revolve

Faithfully, without going astray.

ཚེས་གསུམ་ཟླ་བ་དཀར་ཁ། །

དཀར་གྱིས་ནང་ནས་ཆོད་སོང་། །

བཙོ་ལྕི་ཡི་ནས་དང་མཉམ་པའི། །

ཞལ་བཞེས་ཅིག་ཀྱང་གནང་ཞུ། །

ས་བཅུའི་དབྱིངས་སུ་བཞུགས་པའི། །

དམ་ཅན་རྡོ་རྗེ་ཆོས་སྐྱོང་། །

མཐུ་དང་ནུས་བ་ཡོད་ན། །

བསྟན་པའི་དགྲ་བོ་སྒྲོལ་དང་། །

Like the rising moon of the third day

My beloved is dressed pure and white,

But on the full moon of the fifteenth
day

Take an oath of meeting as pure and
bright.

The transcendent *Dorje Choskyong*,

The oracle of the Tenth Spiritual Stage,

If you have supernatural powers

Destroy the foes of the *dharma*.

ཁྱུ་ཕྱུག་མོན་ནས་འོངས་པས། །
གནམ་ལོའི་ས་བཅུད་འཕལ་སོང་། །
ང་དང་བྱམས་པ་ཕྱུད་ནས། །
ལུས་སེམས་སྟིད་པོར་ལངས་སོང་། །

ཁྱི་རེ་སྔག་ཁྱི་གཟིག་ཁྱི། །
མདའ་ཁ་སྟེར་ནས་འདྲེས་སོང་། །
ནང་གི་སྔག་མོ་རས་འརྫོམས། །
འདྲེས་ནས་མཐུར་དུ་ལང་སོང་། །

The cuckoo returns

From the land of *Mon**

Bringing rains for the dry fields.

I have now met my beloved,

I relax in bliss and tranquillity.

Dogs of any kind

Can be tamed with meat and bread;

But the tigress of the tavern, even when
    tamed,

Rises viciously and rebels again.

*Refers to Tawang in north-eastern India, the birthplace of the
Sixth Dalai Lama.

ཤ་འཇམ་ལུས་པོ་འདྲིས་ཀྱང་། །

བྱམས་པའི་གདེང་ཚོད་མི་ལོན། །

ས་ལ་རེ་མོ་བྲིས་པས། །

ནམ་མཁའི་སྐར་ཚོད་ཐིག་བྱུང་། །

ང་དང་བྱམས་པའི་སྙིབས་ས། །

ཀླུ་རོང་སྤྱིན་པའི་ནགས་གསེབ། །

སྨྲ་མཁན་ནེ་ཙོ་མ་གཏོགས། །

སུ་དང་གང་གིས་མི་ཤེས། །

སྨྲ་མཁན་ནེ་ཙོ་ཨོ་ཤེས། །

གསང་ཁ་སྟོན་པ་མ་གནང་། །

Even the stars in the sky

Can be measured by astrology.

Her body can be caressed,

But not so fathomed

Her deep inner longing.

I secretly meet my beloved

In the forest of the southern valley.

At gossip corners, the talkative parrot

Must stop revealing the secret of my
affair.

ལྷ་ས་མི་རྟོགས་མ་བྱུག་ལ། །

ཅུང་ཅུལ་མི་སྲུས་དཀའ་པ། །

ང་ལ་ཡོད་པའི་ཅུང་འདྲེས། །

ཅུང་ཅུལ་གཞུང་ན་ཡོད་དོ། །

ཁྱི་ནན་ཅུ་འུ་ཟེར་བ། །

རྣམ་ཤེས་མི་ལས་སྐྱུང་བ། །

སྲོད་ལ་ལྡངས་སོང་མ་ཟེར། །

ཐོ་རངས་ལྱོག་བྱུང་མ་ཟེར། །

In Lhasa the crowd is dense

But in Chungyal the crowd is charm-
ing.

My sweetheart whom I long for

Is now in Chungyal valley.

The old dog at guard

Has a soul more cunning than humans.

Do not tell people:

"At dusk he left and at dawn he returned."

སྦྱིན་ལ་ཕྱུགས་པ་བཙལ་བའི། །

ཁ་བ་མང་པོ་འབབ་བྱུང་། །

གསང་དང་མ་གསང་མི་འདུག །

ཞབས་རྗེས་གངས་ལ་བཞག་གི །

པོ་ཏུ་ལ་རུ་བཞུགས་དུས། །

རིག་འཛིན་ཚངས་དབྱངས་རྒྱ་མཚོ། །

ལྷ་ས་ཞོལ་དུ་སྒྱིད་དུས། །

འཆེལ་པོ་དང་བཟང་དབང་པོ། །

It snowed at dusk

When I searched for my sweetheart.

Now the secret cannot be kept;

In the snow my footprints remain.

When I dwell in the Potala

I am *Rigdzin Tsangyang Gyatso*,

When I roam in Lhasa and Shol

I am the libertine, *Dangzang Wangpo*.

ཁ་འཛུམ་མལ་ས་ནང་གི། །

སྙིང་སྲུག་དུང་སེམས་ཅན་མ། །

ཨི་ལོས་དགེ་རོར་འཕྲོགས་པའི། །

གཡོ་སྐྱུ་བཀད་པ་མིན་འགྲོ། །

དབུ་ཞུ་དབུ་ལ་བཞེས་སོང་། །

དབུ་ལྕང་རྒྱབ་ལ་དབྱུགས་སོང་། །

ག་ལེར་ཡེ་བབས་ཤིག་བྱུས་པས། །

ག་ལེར་བཞུགས་ཤིག་གསུང་གི། །

བྱུགས་སེམས་སྐྱུ་ཡོང་བྱུས་པས། །

མ་ཁྱིགས་པོ་འཕྲུད་ཡོང་གསུངས་བྱུང་། །

90

49

Sweetheart awaiting me in my bed

Yielding tenderly her sweet soft body,

Has she come to cheat me

And disrobe me of my virtues?

50

She left wearing her hat,

Slinging her hair back,

Bidding farewell.

"It's sad to say farewell," I said.

"Do not be sad, my love," she said,

"After every parting

Comes another meeting."

མདའ་མོ་འབེན་ལ་ཕོགས་སོང་། །

མའི་བུ་ས་ལ་འཇུལ་སོང་། །

རྒྱང་འདྲེས་བྱམས་པ་འཕུད་བྱུང་། །

སེམས་ཉིད་རྗེས་ལ་འབྱང་སོང་། །

རྒྱ་གར་ཤར་གྱི་རྨ་བྱ། །

ཁོང་ཡུལ་མཐིལ་གྱི་ནེ་ཙོ། །

འབྱུངས་ས་འབྱུངས་ཡུལ་མི་གཅིག །

འཛོམས་ས་ཆོས་འཁོར་ལྷ་ས། །

The arrow has hit the target,

Its point has cut into the earth.

I have met my beloved.

My heart follows her, all by itself.

Peacocks from eastern India,

Parrot from the depths of Kongpo,

Though born in separate countries

Finally come together

In the holy land of Lhasa.

མི་ཚོང་ལ་ལབ་པ། །

དགོངས་སུ་དགག་པ་ཁག་ཐེག །

ཨོ་ལོའི་གོམ་གསུམ་ཕྱུ་མོ། །

གནས་མོའི་ནང་ལ་ཐལ་སོང་། །

ལྕང་མ་ཕྱེ་འུར་སེམས་ཕོར། །

ཕྱེའུ་ལྕང་མར་སེམས་ཕོར། །

སེམས་ཕོར་མཐུན་པ་བྱུང་ན། །

སྐུ་ཁྲ་ཆོར་བས་མི་ཐུབ། །

People gossip about me.

I am sorry for what I have done;

I have taken three thin steps

And landed myself in the tavern of my
mistress.

The willow is in love with the sparrow

And the sparrow is in love with the
willow.

When the willow and the sparrow love
each other,

What can the grey hawk do to enchant
the sparrow?

དང་ལྕའི་ཁྱི་འབྱུང་འདི་ལ། །

དེ་ཁ་ཚམ་ཞིག་ཞུས་ནས། །

གཏིང་མ་ཕྱིས་པའི་ལོ་ལ། །

མཛལ་འརྟོ་མས་ཨེ་ཡོང་བལྟོའོ། །

བུ་དེ་སྨྲ་མཁན་ནེ་ཙོ། །

ཁ་རོགས་བཞུགས་རོགས་མཛོད་དང་། །

ལྕང་སྒྱིང་ཨ་ཙེ་འརྟོལ་མོས། །

གསུང་སྐྱེན་སྐྱར་དགོས་བྱུང་། །

In the short walk of this life

We have had our share of joy.

Let us hope to meet again

In the youth of our next life.

The garrulous parrot

Please stay with your mouth shut.

The thrush in the willow grove

Has promised to sing a song for me.

ཅུབ་ཀྱི་སྐྱ་བདུད་བཙན་པོ། །

འཇིགས་དང་མི་འཇིགས་མི་འདུག །

མདུན་གྱི་ཀཱ་ར་ཀུ་རུ། །

ཐིགས་སུ་དགས་པ་བྱས་སོང་། །

བྱེ་ཁྱུང་ཁྱུང་དཀར་མོ། །

ང་ལ་གཤོག་རྩལ་གཡར་དང་། །

ཐག་རིང་བསྐྱངས་ལ་མི་འགྲོ། །

ཡི་ཐང་བསྐོར་ནས་སྐྱེབས་ཡོང་། །

Though the devil thorns at the back are
  fierce,

The apples in the front are ripe.

Though scared of the devil thorns,

I have decided once and for all

To pluck the ripe apples in front of me.

White crane!

Lend me your wings.

I shall not fly far;

From Lithang, I shall return.

ཤི་རེ་དཀྱིལ་བའི་ཡུལ་གྱི་རེ་རེ། །

ཆོས་རྒྱལ་ལས་ཀྱི་མེ་ལོང་། །

འདི་ན་ཁྲིག་ཁྲིག་མི་འདུག །

དེ་ནས་ཁྲིག་ཁྲིག་གཏང་ཞུ། །

Yama, the mirror of my *karma*

Residing in the realm of death,

You must judge and grant justice.

Here, while alive, I had no justice.

Gedhun